Simpson

AF215059

by Iain Gray

PUBLISHING

WRITING *to* REMEMBER

LangSyne
PUBLISHING
WRITING *to* REMEMBER

79 Main Street, Newtongrange,
Midlothian EH22 4NA
Tel: 0131 344 0414
E-mail: info@lang-syne.co.uk
www.langsyneshop.co.uk

Design by Dorothy Meikle
Printed by Printwell Ltd
© Lang Syne Publishers Ltd 2023

All rights reserved. No part of this publication may be reproduced, stored
or introduced into a retrieval system, or transmitted in any form or by any
means (electronic, mechanical, photocopying, recording or otherwise) without
the prior written permission of Lang Syne Publishers Ltd.

ISBN 978-1-85217-598-6

Simpson

MOTTO:
Never despairing.

CREST:
A demi-lion.

NAME variations include:
Simpsone
Simsoun

Chapter one:

The origins of popular surnames

by George Forbes and Iain Gray

If you don't know where you came from, you won't know where you're going **is a frequently quoted observation and one that has a particular resonance today when there has been a marked upsurge in interest in genealogy, with increasing numbers of people curious to trace their family roots.**

Main sources for genealogical research include census returns and official records of births, marriages and deaths – and the key to unlocking the detail they contain is obviously a family surname, one that has been 'inherited' and passed from generation to generation.

No matter our station in life, we all have a surname – but it was not until about the middle of the fourteenth century that the practice of being identified by a particular surname became commonly established throughout the British Isles.

Previous to this, it was normal for a person to be identified through the use of only a forename.

But as population gradually increased and there were many more people with the same forename, surnames were adopted to distinguish one person, or community, from another.

Many common English surnames are patronymic in origin, meaning they stem from the forename of one's father – with 'Johnson,' for example, indicating 'son of John.'

It was the Normans, in the wake of their eleventh century conquest of Anglo-Saxon England, a pivotal moment in the nation's history, who first brought surnames into usage – although it was a gradual process.

For the Normans, these were names initially based on the title of their estates, local villages and chateaux in France to distinguish and identify these landholdings.

Such grand descriptions also helped enhance the prestige of these warlords and generally glorify their lofty positions high above the humble serfs slaving away below in the pecking order who had only single names, often with Biblical connotations as in Pierre and Jacques.

The only descriptive distinctions among the peasantry concerned their occupations, like 'Pierre the swineherd' or 'Jacques the ferryman.'

Roots of surnames that came into usage in England not only included Norman-French, but also Old French, Old Norse, Old English, Middle English, German, Latin, Greek, Hebrew and the Gaelic languages of the Celts.

The Normans themselves were originally Vikings, or 'Northmen', who raided, colonised and eventually settled down around the French coastline.

They had sailed up the Seine in their long-boats in 900AD under their ferocious leader Rollo and ruled the roost in north eastern France before sailing over to conquer England in 1066 under Duke William of Normandy – better known to posterity as William the Conqueror, or King William I of England.

Granted lands in the newly-conquered England, some of their descendants later acquired territories in Wales, Scotland and Ireland – taking not only their own surnames, but also the practice of adopting a surname, with them.

But it was in England where Norman rule and custom first impacted, particularly in relation to the adoption of surnames.

This is reflected in the famous *Domesday Book*, a massive survey of much of England and Wales, ordered by William I, to determine who owned what, what it was worth and therefore how much they were liable to pay in taxes to the voracious Royal Exchequer.

Completed in 1086 and now held in the National Archives in Kew, London, 'Domesday' was an Old English word meaning 'Day of Judgement.'

This was because, in the words of one contemporary chronicler, "its decisions, like those of the Last Judgement, are unalterable."

It had been a requirement of all those English landholders – from the richest to the poorest – that they identify themselves for the purposes of the survey and for future reference by means of a surname.

This is why the *Domesday Book*, although written in Latin as was the practice for several centuries with both civic and ecclesiastical records, is an invaluable source for the early appearance of a wide range of English surnames.

Several of these names were coined in connection with occupations.

These include Baker and Smith, while Cooks, Chamberlains, Constables and Porters were to be found carrying out duties in large medieval households.

The church's influence can be found in names such as Bishop, Friar and Monk while the popular name of Bennett derives from the late fifth to mid-sixth century Saint Benedict, founder of the Benedictine order of monks.

The early medical profession is represented by Barber, while businessmen produced names that include Merchant and Sellers.

Down at the village watermill, the names that cropped up included Millar/Miller, Walker and Fuller, while other self-explanatory trades included Cooper, Tailor, Mason and Wright.

Even the scenery was utilised as in Moor, Hill, Wood and Forrest – while the hunt and the chase supplied names that include Hunter, Falconer, Fowler and Fox.

Colours are also a source of popular surnames, as in Black, Brown, Gray/Grey, Green and White, and would have denoted the colour of the clothing the person habitually wore or, apart from the obvious exception of 'Green', one's hair colouring or even complexion.

The surname Red developed into Reid, while

Blue was rare and no-one wanted to be associated with yellow.

Rather self-important individuals took surnames that include Goodman and Wiseman, while physical attributes crept into surnames such as Small and Little.

Many families proudly boast the heraldic device known as a Coat of Arms, as featured on our front cover.

The central motif of the Coat of Arms would originally have been what was borne on the shield of a warrior to distinguish himself from others on the battlefield.

Not featured on the Coat of Arms, but high-lighted on page three, is the family motto and related crest – with the latter frequently different from the central motif.

Adding further variety to the rich cultural heritage that is represented by surnames is the appearance in recent times in lists of the 100 most common names found in England of ones that include Khan, Patel and Singh – names that have proud roots in the vast sub-continent of India.

Echoes of a far distant past can still be found in our surnames and they can be borne with pride in commemoration of our forebears.

Chapter two:

Saxons and Normans

Ranked 67th in some lists of the 100 most popular surnames found in England today, 'Simpson' derives from the given name 'Simon' – that in turn originates from the Hebrew 'Shimeon', denoting 'obedience.'

Of ancient roots, the ancestry of many present day English bearers of the name stretches back through the dim mists of time to the Anglo-Saxons, specifically the Saxons.

This means that flowing through the veins of many bearers of the name today may well be the blood of those Germanic tribes who invaded and settled in the south and east of the island of Britain from about the early fifth century.

Known as the Anglo-Saxons, they were composed of the Jutes, from the area of the Jutland Peninsula in modern Denmark, the Saxons from Lower Saxony, in modern Germany and the Angles from the Angeln area of Germany.

It was on the eastern coast that the Angles first settled – later giving the name 'Engla land', or 'Aengla land' – better known as 'England' – while the

Saxons were found in the south, particularly in what is the modern day south-eastern county of Kent.

It is in Kent that the forebears of those who would later take the Simpson name were first found.

The Anglo-Saxons held sway from approximately 550 to 1066, with the main kingdoms those of Sussex, Wessex, Northumbria, Mercia, East Anglia, Essex and the early Simpson homeland of Kent.

Whoever controlled the most powerful of these kingdoms was tacitly recognised as overall 'king' – one of the most noted being Alfred the Great, King of Wessex from 871 to 899.

It was during his reign that the famous *Anglo-Saxon Chronicle* was compiled – an invaluable source of Anglo-Saxon history – while Alfred was designated in early documents as *Rex Anglorum Saxonum*, King of the English Saxons.

Other Anglo-Saxon works include the epic *Beowulf* and the seventh century *Caedmon's Hymn*.

The Anglo-Saxons, meanwhile, had usurped the power of the indigenous Britons – who referred to them as 'Saeson' or 'Saxones.'

But the death knell of Anglo-Saxon supremacy was sounded with the Norman Conquest of 1066, a pivotal event in England's history.

By this date, it had become a nation with several powerful competitors to the throne.

In what were extremely complex family, political and military machinations, the monarch was Harold II, who had succeeded to the throne following the death of Edward the Confessor.

But his right to the throne was contested by two powerful competitors – his brother-in-law King Harold Hardrada of Norway, in alliance with Tostig, Harold II's brother, and Duke William II of Normandy.

In what has become known as The Year of Three Battles, Hardrada invaded England and gained victory over the English king on September 20 at the battle of Fulford, in Yorkshire.

Five days later, however, Harold II decisively defeated his brother-in-law and brother at the battle of Stamford Bridge.

But he had little time to celebrate his victory, having to immediately march south from Yorkshire to encounter a mighty invasion force, led by Duke William, that had landed at Hastings, in East Sussex.

Harold's battle-hardened but exhausted force of Anglo-Saxon soldiers confronted the Normans on October 14 in a battle subsequently depicted on the Bayeux tapestry – a 23ft. long strip of embroidered linen thought to have been commissioned eleven years after the event by the Norman Odo of Bayeux.

Harold drew up a strong defensive position, at the top of Senlac Hill, building a shield wall to repel Duke William's cavalry and infantry.

The Normans suffered heavy losses, but through a combination of the deadly skill of their archers and the ferocious determination of their cavalry they eventually won the day.

Anglo-Saxon morale had collapsed on the battlefield as word spread through the ranks that Harold, the last of the Anglo-Saxon kings, had been killed – the Bayeux Tapestry depicting this as having happened when he was struck by an arrow to the head.

William was declared King of England on December 25, and the subjugation of his Anglo-Saxon subjects followed.

Those Normans who had fought on his behalf were rewarded with the lands of Anglo-Saxons and, within an astonishingly short space of time, Norman manners, customs and law were imposed on England – laying the basis for what subsequently became established 'English' custom and practice.

Meanwhile, a family of those who would later take the Simpson surname had more than 100 years before the Conquest moved from Kent to present day Buckinghamshire, and it is with this county that they are particularly identified.

They family, tracing a descent from a Saxon lord known as Archil, were somehow able to reach an accommodation with their Norman overlords and managed to retain much of their lands – and are recorded in the *Domesday Book* of 1086, referred to in *Chapter One*.

Their landholdings also included the manor of Clint, in Yorkshire, where they established a main seat at Castle Lodge.

They adopted the name 'de Clint', but at some point in the twelfth century descendants of Simon de Clint, son of William de Clint, adopted the 'Simpson' surname in order to distinguish themselves from the other 'de Clints.'

Branches of the de Clints/Simpsons meanwhile 'migrated' to Scotland, acquiring new lands in Fifeshire, specifically at Brunton, and forging a close kinship with Clan Fraser.

In England, the Simpsons continued to flourish with, in addition to their Yorkshire land holdings, the estates of Mellor Lodge, in Derby, and Bradley, in Durham.

Chapter three:

Royalty and research

One particularly colourful and controversial bearer of the Simpson name was Wallis Simpson, later Duchess of Windsor, who caused a British constitutional crisis in the 1930s when King Edward VIII abdicated in order to marry the divorced American socialite.

Born Bessie Wallis Warfield in 1896, her father Teackle Wallis Warfield was the son of a wealthy Baltimore flour merchant. He died only a few months after his daughter's birth and she and her mother, Alice, became dependant on the charity of her father's brother, S. Davis Warfield.

Later moving into the home of a widowed aunt in Baltimore before acquiring their own home in the city, it was in 1916 while on a visit to Florida that she met the dashing U.S. Navy aviator Earl Winfield Spencer, Jr. The couple married that same year, but divorced in 1927.

Less than a year after the divorce, on a visit to London, she met and married the wealthy Ernest Aldrich Simpson.

Born in 1897 in New York City and a partner in the ship-brokerage firm Simpson, Spence and Young, he had previously renounced his American citizenship and, becoming a naturalised British citizen, served as a captain in the Coldstream Guards during the First World War.

The couple divorced in October of 1936 – while two years previously she had embarked on an affair with the heir to the British throne, Edward, Prince of Wales.

Besotted with 'Mrs Simpson', Edward made no attempt to keep the affair secret, gifting her money and expensive jewellery, holidaying with her and, on one occasion, to the shock of all present, arriving with his lover to an evening party in Buckingham Palace and introducing her to the Queen.

Although reports of the affair were appearing in the foreign press, the British media maintained a deafening and deferential silence.

King George V died in January of 1936 and Edward ascended the throne as King Edward VIII.

In November of that year, the king met with Prime Minister Stanley Baldwin to discuss ways to marry Wallis Simpson and still keep the throne.

The main bar to the marriage was that the

monarch is recognised as the Supreme Governor of the Church of England, and the Church – up until 2002 – did not allow the remarriage of divorced people who had two living ex-spouses, as was the case with the king's intended.

Edward suggested a morganatic marriage, whereby he would remain king but his wife would not be recognised as queen – but the suggestion was rejected by Baldwin and other Commonwealth leaders who had been consulted on the matter.

By this time the British press had at last broken its silence on the affair and the constitutional crisis it entailed – with the king attracting both sympathetic supporters and angry critics. The king, adamant in his desire to marry Wallis, found himself with no option but to relinquish the throne by abdicating.

The Instrument of Abdication was signed on September 10, 1936 and in an emotional radio broadcast the following day, Edward stated: "I have found it impossible to carry the heavy burden of responsibility, and to discharge my duties as king as I would wish to do, without the help and support of the woman I love."

His brother, the Duke of York, duly ascended the throne as George VI and Edward and Wallis married in France in June of 1937 at the Château de Candé, in Monto – with the new king having granted them the titles of Duke and Duchess of Windsor.

The couple lived in France up until the outbreak of the Second World War, while they were accused of harbouring pro-Nazi sympathies following a visit to Germany in 1937 and a controversial meeting with Adolf Hitler at his mountain retreat near Berchtesgaden, Bavaria.

It is unlikely the couple were indeed pro-Nazi, however, otherwise the Duke would not have been given a military post with the British Army in France on the outbreak of war and, later in the conflict, appointed Governor of the Bahamas and with the Duchess as First Lady.

Stationed in the Bahamas throughout the remainder of the war, they spent their remaining years in a mansion in the Bois de Boulogne district of Paris.

The Duke died in 1972 and was buried in the Royal Burial Ground near Windsor Castle.

The Duchess was laid to rest beside him following her death in 1986, while her magnificent collection of jewellery, auctioned by Sotheby's in Geneva in 1987, fetched £45m for the Pasteur Institute Medical Research Foundation.

Going back to the nineteenth century, a huge debt is owed by the medical world to Sir James Young Simpson, born in Bathgate, West Lothian, in 1811, and who pioneered the use of anaesthetics in surgical operations.

A landmark date in the history of medicine is January 19, 1847, when Simpson, who had studied at Edinburgh University, became the first to apply ether as an anaesthetic to reduce the pain of childbirth.

This was during the stern and strict Victorian age, and Simpson had to struggle against those who believed the use of anaesthetics was a crime against God and nature – the vast majority of these opponents, perhaps needless to say, were men. After experimenting with ether, Simpson discovered the anaesthetic properties of chloroform, the use of which became hugely popular after it was administered to Queen Victoria during the delivery of Prince Leopold in 1853.

Aged only 28, Simpson, who became the first person to be knighted for services to medicine, was appointed to the Chair of Midwifery at Edinburgh University while, in addition to radically improving the design of obstetrical forceps, he also pioneered techniques to reduce some of the fatal diseases often associated with childbirth.

Simpson had his own coat of arms, and his great achievements in medicine are aptly summed up in his personal motto of 'Victo Dolore' (Pain Conquered).

Thousands of people gathered for his funeral in Edinburgh, following his death in 1870, and he is buried in the city's Warriston Cemetery.

Another inventive mind and an intrepid researcher was the pioneering British meteorologist Sir George Clarke Simpson, born in 1878 in Derby, the son of a department store proprietor.

Educated at Owens College, Manchester and Göttingen University, Germany, he travelled to Lapland in 1902 to investigate the phenomenon of atmospheric electricity and three years later was appointed lecturer in meteorology at Manchester University – the first such appointment at a British University.

By 1906 he was in India with the Indian Meteorological Service, based at Simla, but his greatest challenge came in 1910 when he was appointed the meteorologist for Captain Robert Falcon Scott's ill-fated *Terra Nova Expedition* to the Antarctic, with *Terra Nova* the name of their ship. Despite the harsh weather conditions on Antarctica, Simpson managed to maintain a cheerful disposition – hence the nickname of "Sunny Jim" that was bestowed on him by the other members of the expedition.

Conducting balloon experiments to test the atmosphere, he laid the foundations for research into how temperature is affected by altitude while he also constructed one of Antarctica's first weather stations, at the expedition's base camp at Cape Evans.

The Royal Geographical Society, organisers of the expedition, had stated before the *Terra Nova* sailed that its main objective was "scientific primarily, with exploration and the South Pole as secondary objects."

Scott, however, aware that his Norwegian rival Roald Amundsen was on his way to attempt to reach the Pole, stated that as far as he was concerned his main objective was "to reach the South Pole, and to secure for the British Empire the honour of this achievement."

Simpson remained at base camp, carrying out his weather experiments, while Scott, along with four others – Henry Bowers, Edgar Evans, Lawrence Oates and Edward Wilson – did indeed reach the Pole, on January 12, 1912, but only to find Amundsen's party had beaten them to it by about five weeks.

Making their dispirited way back to base

camp – exhausted, frozen and with their supplies all but depleted – Oates voluntarily left their tent and walked to his death with the farewell: "I am just going out and may be some time."

The rest of the party quickly succumbed to the terrible conditions, with Scott believed to have died on about March 29. Their bodies were discovered by a search party on November 29, and buried where they had made camp.

Returning from Antarctica with the other surviving members of the expedition, Simpson rejoined the Indian Meteorological Service, and it was in his spare time that he completed a detailed report on the valuable meteorological data he had gathered while in the frozen wastes.

Appointed director of the Meteorological Office, London, he served in this post until his retirement in 1938, three years after he had been knighted, carrying out research into solar radiation, ionization, atmospheric electricity and the causes of lightning.

He also established what is now known as the Simpson Wind Force Scale, a modification of the Beaufort Scale, while he was called out of retirement during the Second World War to take charge of Kew

Observatory. Remaining at Kew until 1947, where he had continued research into meteorological fields such as the electrical structure of thunderstorms, he died in 1965.

Yet another intrepid bearer of the Simpson name was George Simpson, born out of wedlock in about 1787 and raised by an aunt in Dingwall, in the north of Scotland, and who overcame the disadvantages of his birth to become governor of the Hudson Bay Company in Canada and achieve the accolade of knighthood.

He left his native Scotland to work in an uncle's sugar brokerage in London, later obtaining a post with the North West Company.

Simpson was entrusted with one of the company's trading posts in Canada and, following the merger of the company with the Hudson Bay Company, he was appointed governor.

In addition to his duties as governor of the Hudson Bay Company, a post he held until 1856, Simpson explored vast tracts of Arctic Canada and from 1841 to 1842 made an arduous and celebrated expedition from Canada, across the inhospitable terrain of Siberia, to St. Petersburg; he died in 1860.

Chapter four:

On the world stage

One particularly infamous bearer of the otherwise proud name of Simpson and one who has suffered a spectacular fall from acclaim is the former top American football player, broadcaster and actor Orenthal James Simpson, better known as O. J. Simpson and also nicknamed "The Juice."

Born in San Francisco in 1947, he was awarded an athletic scholarship to the University of Southern California, where he played in the position of running back in 1967 and 1968.

Taking up football as a career, he played for the Buffalo Bills in 1973 and, later playing for two seasons with the San Francisco 49ers, he was elected to the Pro Football Hall of Fame.

Before his retirement from the game, he had already embarked on an equally successful career as a football broadcaster and actor.

Television credits include the 1977 miniseries *Roots*, while big screen credits include the 1974 *The Klansman* and, in the same year, *The Towering*

Inferno, in addition to the 1988, 1991 and 1994 *The Naked Gun* comedy trilogy.

Previously married to Marguerite Whitley, he had three children – one of whom drowned in the family swimming pool in 1979.

The couple divorced in that same year and in 1985 he married Nicole Brown, with whom he had two children.

He separated from her four years after their marriage, pleading 'no contest' to a charge of domestic violence and the couple divorced in 1992.

In June of 1994, Nicole and her friend Ron Goldman were found stabbed to death outside her Los Angeles home.

Five days after the murders, Simpson failed to turn himself into the police, as had been requested.

He became the subject of a pursuit – captured live on television through a camera-equipped helicopter as he sped from the police in his Ford Bronco SUV in an abortive attempt to evade them.

Brought to trial, with the proceedings televised live across the world, in October of 1995 a jury acquitted him of the murders.

Two years later, however, in a civil action brought by the families of the murder victims, he was found guilty of their 'wrongful deaths' and ordered to pay out a total of $33.5m to the families.

In September of 2007, Simpson again came to international media attention when he was arrested in Las Vegas and charged with a number of crimes that included kidnap and armed robbery.

He was found guilty in 2008 and sentenced to 33 years' imprisonment, with a minimum of nine years without parole.

The former star of the football field and the screen is now serving his sentence at the Lovelock Correction Center, Nevada.

From infamy to contemporary fame, James Raymond Simpson, better known as **Jimmi Simpson**, is the American actor of stage, television and film whose portrayal of Philo T. Farnsworth in the Broadway production of *The Farnsworth Invention* won him a World Theatre Award.

Born in 1975 in Hackettstown, New Jersey, his many television credits include *House of Cards*, *CSI: Crime Scene Investigation*, *24* and *My Name is Earl*, while big screen credits include the 2000 *Loser*, the 2005 *Herbie: Fully Loaded*, the 2012 *Abraham Lincoln: Vampire Hunter* and, from 2013, *White House Down*.

On British shores, William Nicholson Simpson was the Scottish actor better known as **Bill Simpson**.

Born in 1931 in Dunure, Ayrshire, he is best known for his role of Dr Alan Finlay in the television medical drama *Dr Finlay's Casebook*, based on the books by A. J. Cronin.

Set in the fictional village of Tannochbrae, and with locations filmed in Callander, Stirlingshire, the popular series ran from 1962 to 1971 with Andrew Cruickshank as Dr Cameron and Barbara Mullen as their housekeeper Janet.

The actor, who also featured in 104 audio episodes for BBC Radio 4 of *The A. J. Cronin Story* and the 1973 television drama *Scotch on the Rocks*, died in 1986.

Also on British television screens, John Cody-Fidler Simpson is the BBC foreign correspondent and world affairs editor better known as **John Simpson**.

The colourful explanation as to why 'Cody' appears in his surname goes back to his great grandmother Elizabeth Mary King, who left her husband Edward King for the famous Wild West showman Samuel Franklin Cowdrey – better known to posterity as Samuel Franklin Cody.

Cody's marriage to his American wife had never been legally dissolved, but he and Simpson's great grandmother lived together as man and wife while she and their sons appeared in Cody's popular demonstrations of lassoing, shooting and horse riding.

Born in Lincoln in 1944, Simpson, a graduate of Magdalene College, Cambridge, joined BBC radio news in 1966 as a trainee sub-editor, becoming a reporter four years later.

Political editor for the BBC from 1980 to 1981 and presenter of its flagship *Nine O'Clock News* from 1981 to 1982, he was appointed BBC world affairs editor in 1988.

His many foreign exploits include being present at the Tiananmen Square massacre in Beijing in 1989 and reporting from Belgrade during the Kosovo War of 1999, while in 2001, wearing a burqa for disguise, he was one of the first reporters to enter Afghanistan during the U.S. invasion of the country and to subsequently report from Kabul.

The recipient of a number of honours and awards that include a CBE, an International Emmy for his report on the fall of Kabul, and three BAFTAS, he is also the author of books that include his

1990 *Despatches from the Barricades* and the 2010 *Unreliable Sources*.

Behind the camera lens, **Alan Simpson**, born in 1929, is one half, along with Ray Galton, of the British scriptwriting partnership **Galton and Simpson**.

First working on radio variety scripts and later television scripts between 1954 and 1961 for comedian Tony Hancock, they are also known for the television situation comedy *Steptoe and Son* that ran from 1962 to 1974.

Also writers between 1961 and 1962 of the *Comedy Playhouse* series for the BBC, both are recipients of an OBE for their contribution to British television.

The duo, meanwhile, had first met in 1948 while recuperating from tuberculosis at Milford Sanatorium near Godalming, Surrey.

The sanatorium is now Milford Hospital – where in 2013 the British Comedy Society unveiled a blue plaque to them in recognition of their historic first meeting.

In the world of music, **Ashlee Simpson**, born in 1984 in Waco, Texas, is the American singer, songwriter and actress whose 2004 debut album

Autobiography reached the top of the U.S. album charts, as did her 2005 *I Am Me*.

She is the younger sister of the singer and actress **Jessica Simpson**, whose best-selling albums include her 1999 *Sweet Kisses* and the 2003 *In This Skin*. She also had her own television reality show, *Newlyweds: Nick and Jessica*, in which her sister Ashlee also participated.

Descended through his mother from the nineteenth century English pianist, conductor and composer Sir William Sterndale Bennett, Charles Simpson, better known as **Charlie Simpson**, is a former lead guitarist with the BRIT Award-winning band Busted.

Born in 1985 in Woodbridge, Suffolk, he had top selling hits with the band that include their 2002 *What I Go to School For* and the 2003 *Crashed the Wedding*, while he later formed the band Fightstar.

Born in 1975 in Denver, Colorado, India Arie Simpson is the award-winning American singer, songwriter, musician and record producer better known as **India.Arie**.

Her albums include her 2001 *Acoustic Soul*, certified double platinum by the Recording Industry Association of America (RIAA).

Along with her husband Nickolas Ashford, **Valerie Simpson**, born in 1946 in The Bronx, New York, was a member of the songwriting partnership Ashley and Simpson.

Before Ashford's death in 2011, the couple were responsible for writing a string of memorable songs that include *Ain't No Mountain High Enough*, a hit in 1967 for Marvin Gaye and Tammi Terrell and later for Diana Ross.

Their *Reach Out and Touch (Somebody's Hand)* was a hit for Diana Ross in 1970, and *I'm Every Woman* a hit for Chaka Khan in 1978.

Also performers in their own right, with hits that include their 1984 *Solid (As a Rock)*, they were inducted into the Songwriters Hall of Fame in 2002.

Bearers of the Simpson name have also excelled in the highly competitive world of sport.

On the fields of European football, **Jimmie Simpson**, born in 1908, was the Scottish international player who, playing for Rangers during the 1930s, won five League Championships and four Scottish Cups.

He died in 1972, while he was the father of the Scottish goalkeeper **Ronnie Simpson**.

Born in Glasgow in 1930, he is best remembered as having been a member of the famous

Celtic team dubbed the Lisbon Lions – who in 1967 became the first British team to win the European Cup.

He died in 2004, seven years before being posthumously inducted into the Scottish Football Hall of Fame.

Meanwhile no mention of the Simpsons could perhaps be complete without reference to the Simpson family – the cartoon characters who since 1989 have featured in the American animated television series **The Simpsons**.

Created by cartoonist Matt Groening, the popular series features the hapless Homer Simpson, his wife Marge and their three children Bart, Lisa and Maggie.